Out of the Darkness:

Escaping Domestic Violence and Embracing a Life of Peace

Dr. Latina C. Campbell

Print ISBN: 978-1-955312-82-0

eBook ISBN: 978-1-955312-83-7

Printed in the United States of America

Story Corner Publishing & Consulting, Inc.

Chesapeake, VA 23321

Storycornerpublishing@yahoo.com

www.StoryCornerPublishing.com

Dedication

I dedicate this book to all the women trying to find a way out. Put together a plan, move quickly, and don't look back! You can do this. I am a living testimony.

Table of Contents

Introduction

I remember feeling trapped on the Ferris wheel of life, unsure of how to escape. Every day, my mind was plagued by thoughts of suicide. I longed for more but constantly settled for less. No matter how hard I tried, I found myself stuck in a cycle of relationships with men who didn't truly love me. How was this possible? Was I not worthy of love? Was I doing something wrong?

When I was younger, my parents separated, and it shook my world. I felt as though the solid ground beneath my feet had vanished. Trauma crept in, and anxiety followed. I began to fear the unknown, convinced that every good thing in my life would eventually be taken away. Yet, I desperately longed to feel love again. My heart felt empty, and I sought to fill it by any means. As I grew older and started dating, I thought I was content, but deep down, I knew it wasn't what I was looking for. A few heartbreaks came, but I assumed that was just part of life.

Years later, my dad passed away, and my world came crashing down. A part of me died with him, and I struggled to figure out how to keep living. The thought of giving up crossed my mind, but by then, I was a single mother. I knew I had to live for my child. With little support, I found myself navigating life alone. My goal was clear: to raise my child better than I had seen and give her the best life possible. I rolled up my sleeves and began working on my dreams—until I met "him."

He seemed different. He was charming, spontaneous, and knew exactly what to say to make me feel safe. I believed he had my back—until he didn't. His true nature revealed itself, and I was caught in a nightmare. He transformed into someone unrecognizable, leaving me frightened for my life. Just when I thought I could break free, I found out I was pregnant. That changed everything. I doubted myself, questioning if I had been overreacting, and stayed, hoping he would change. After all, we were going to have a child together.

But things only got worse. He believed my pregnancy meant I would endure anything. Knowing I didn't want to be a single mother of two, he used my longing for a family against me. The abuse escalated—emotional, mental, spiritual, and even physical. When I finally saw how heartless he was, I realized I had to stop waiting for him to become someone he wasn't. I had to leave, not just for myself but for my children. I couldn't let them grow up in that environment. It was a hard conclusion to reach, but I knew I deserved better.

I had to be strategic. He was intelligent and manipulative, even ensuring there were no visible scars from his abuse. On the surface, he was a respected professional with a prestigious job, so who would believe me? I later discovered he had fathered 17 children with 17 other women, ruining each of their lives. While I was pregnant, two other women were expecting his children as well. He was a master manipulator, believing his own lies.

I began researching him, uncovering truths I wished I had known before. I had been distracted by his love bombing, mistaking manipulation for love. When I finally decided to leave, he oscillated between begging me to stay and threatening me not to go. My exit plan was simple: achieve financial stability, move away, and establish a court-ordered parenting agreement. But God had other plans.

I found a part-time job, applied for assistance, and moved away. Though I should have stuck to my plan, I allowed him visitation before the courts got involved. That's when he used our daughter as a pawn, threatening I'd never see her again because I didn't deserve "his" money for child support. When I called the police, they couldn't act without a court order. It was one of the most terrifying moments of my life.

In that moment of despair, God stepped in. A peace unlike anything I'd ever known washed over me. I told him he could keep our daughter until the court date, but he suddenly changed his mind. He didn't truly want her; he just wanted to hurt me. Seeing that his manipulation no longer affected me, he relented. I knew it was only God who made that possible.

Months later, God met me in an unexpected way at my job. I accepted Him with open arms, and He transformed my life. God swept me off my feet and my heart was filled. Today, I'm married, raising eight children, and running multiple businesses and ministries all thanks to God. The love I searched so desperately for was never missing—God had been with me all along. He was simply waiting for me to let Him in and take control.

Now, God is the foundation of my life, and His love is unmatched. I encourage you to seek Him too. Make your exit plan, trust God to guide you, and know that you deserve better.

Only God can fill the voids in your life and lead you to a brighter future. Accept Him today—you won't regret it.

"If you declare with your mouth, "Jesus is Lord,"and believe in your heart that God raised him from the dead, you will be saved." Romans 10:9 NIV.

The Path to Freedom

Domestic violence is a devastating reality that affects millions of people—women, men, and children—across every social, economic, and cultural background. It is a silent epidemic that thrives in the shadows, fueled by fear, isolation, and shame. If you are in an abusive relationship, know this: you are not alone, and you are not powerless. God sees you, loves you, and wants to lead you to a place of safety, healing, and freedom.

This book is written for you, whether you are a victim or someone supporting a loved one trapped in an abusive situation. It is a guide to help you recognize the abuse for what it is, take courageous steps to leave, and rebuild a life of wholeness with God at the center. The journey out of abuse is neither quick nor easy, but it is possible. With the right support, planning, and faith, you can escape the chains of domestic violence and embrace a life filled with peace, joy, and security.

Why This Book is Necessary

Domestic violence goes beyond physical harm. It can manifest in many forms:

- **Mental abuse**, where the abuser manipulates and gaslights you into doubting your worth and sanity.

- **Emotional abuse**, where words and actions are weaponized to destroy your confidence and sense of self.

- **Spiritual abuse**, where faith is twisted to control or condemn you, making you feel unworthy of God's love.

- **Physical abuse**, where violence is used to dominate and instill fear.

- **Financial abuse**, where control of money is used to trap you in the relationship.

Abuse leaves scars that run deep, often eroding your ability to trust yourself, others, or even God. This book is here to help you reclaim what has been taken from you—your voice, your dignity, your faith, and your future.

God's Heart for the Abused

God never intended for anyone to live in fear or oppression. Throughout scripture, God speaks of His care for the brokenhearted and His desire to deliver the oppressed:

- *"The Lord is a refuge for the oppressed, a stronghold in times of trouble."* (Psalm 9:9)

- *"He heals the brokenhearted and binds up their wounds."* (Psalm 147:3)

- *"Come to me, all you who are weary and burdened, and I will give you rest."* (Matthew 11:28)

These promises are for you. You may feel trapped and hopeless, but God has a way out. He sees your tears, hears your cries, and wants to guide you to freedom.

What You Can Expect from This Book

This book is divided into three parts:

1. **Recognizing Abuse and Building Confidence**: You will learn to identify abusive patterns and how they impact every aspect of your life. You will also discover how to lean on God and rebuild your confidence as His beloved child.

2. **Creating and Executing a Safe Exit Plan**: This section will provide practical steps to leave an abusive relationship safely, especially if children are involved. It includes resources for financial independence, legal considerations, and finding a safe place to stay.

3. **Healing and Living a Fulfilled Life**: After leaving, the journey continues. This part will guide you through emotional and spiritual healing, rebuilding your life, and embracing a future filled with God's peace and purpose.

Who This Book is For

- **Women and Men in Abusive Relationships**: Whether you're married, dating, or cohabiting, this book provides tailored guidance for your situation.

- **Parents with Children**: You will find special focus on how to protect and care for your children while leaving and rebuilding.

- **Supporters of Victims**: If someone you love is in an abusive relationship, this book will help you understand what they're going through and how to support them effectively.

Faith, Action, and Courage

This book is not only about practical steps but also about spiritual transformation. Faith in God is the cornerstone of this journey. Scripture and prayer are woven throughout to remind you that you are not walking this road alone. God's strength will carry you when you feel weak, and His light will guide you out of darkness.

However, faith must be coupled with action. God gives us wisdom and resources to make courageous decisions. This book equips you with both spiritual and practical tools so you can take steps toward freedom while trusting in His divine guidance.

A Final Word of Encouragement

Leaving an abusive relationship is one of the hardest decisions you may ever make. It requires courage, determination, and faith. But know this: you are stronger than you realize, and God's plans for you are good. He wants to restore everything that was stolen from you.

As you begin this journey, remember these words from Isaiah 41:10:
"So do not fear, for I am with you; do not be dismayed, for I am your God. I will strengthen you and help you; I will uphold you with my righteous right hand."

Let this promise be your anchor as you take the first step toward a new, abundant life. You are not alone. God is with you every step of the way. And together, we will walk this path to freedom.

Chapter 1:

Understanding Domestic Violence

Before you can safely leave an abusive relationship, it's important to fully understand the nature of domestic violence and how it impacts every area of your life. Abuse can take many forms, and its effects run deep—mentally, emotionally, spiritually, physically, and financially. Recognizing the signs and acknowledging the reality of your situation are the first steps toward freedom.

What is Domestic Violence?

Domestic violence is a pattern of behavior used to gain or maintain power and control over an intimate partner. It is not just a momentary lapse of anger or frustration but an intentional tactic to dominate another person. Abuse can occur in various forms, sometimes overlapping:

1. **Mental Abuse**: This involves manipulation, gaslighting, and controlling your thoughts and perceptions. You might be made to feel crazy, confused, or incapable of making decisions.

   - *Example*: Your abuser may constantly lie about past events or deny their harmful behavior, making you question your memory and reality.

2. **Emotional Abuse**: This type of abuse undermines your self-esteem and emotional stability. It includes verbal insults, humiliation, intimidation, and neglect.

- *Example*: Being called names, belittled in front of others, or ignored as a way to punish you.

3. **Spiritual Abuse**: Some abusers misuse religion to control or shame their victims. This could involve twisting scripture, using faith to justify abuse, or isolating you from your spiritual community.

- *Example*: "God hates divorce, so you can't leave me," or "You are a bad Christian if you don't forgive me and stay."

4. **Physical Abuse**: This includes any form of violence, such as hitting, choking, pushing, or threatening physical harm. Often, the threat of violence is enough to instill fear.

5. **Financial Abuse**: Controlling your access to money and resources, preventing you from working, or sabotaging your financial independence to keep you dependent.

- *Example*: An abuser may refuse to let you have a bank account, give you an "allowance," or take your earnings for themselves.

Signs You Are in an Abusive Relationship

Abuse is often subtle at first, building gradually over time. Here are some common red flags:

- Your partner isolates you from friends, family, or support systems.

- They monitor your phone, emails, or whereabouts.

- You feel afraid to disagree or express your opinions.

- They blame you for their anger, saying, "You made me do this."

- They withhold affection, money, or necessities as a form of punishment.

- They explode in rage or violence, followed by apologies or promises to change.

Scripture Insight: Abuse is not love. God's design for relationships is based on mutual respect and love, not control or fear. *"There is no fear in love. But perfect love drives out fear."* (1 John 4:18)

The Impact of Abuse

Living in an abusive relationship affects every aspect of your life, even if the wounds are not always visible.

- **Mentally**: Abuse erodes your confidence, leaving you feeling helpless, trapped, and unworthy.

- **Emotionally**: You may experience chronic anxiety, depression, or a sense of hopelessness.

- **Spiritually**: Abuse can shake your faith, making you question God's love or presence.

- **Physically**: Long-term stress can lead to health issues like chronic pain, fatigue, or other medical conditions.

- **Financially**: Abuse often leaves victims without financial resources, making it harder to leave.

Practical Exercise: Take time to journal your thoughts and feelings about your current situation. Reflect on how the relationship makes you feel mentally, emotionally, and spiritually. This can help you see patterns of abuse more clearly.

Why It's Hard to Leave

It's important to understand that leaving an abusive relationship is incredibly difficult for many reasons, including:

- Fear of retaliation or harm to yourself or your children.

- Financial dependency or lack of resources.

- Emotional manipulation, such as guilt-tripping or promises to change.

- Social pressure or stigma, especially within religious or cultural communities.

- Lack of confidence or belief in your ability to survive on your own.

Encouragement: Know that leaving does not mean you are weak or failing—it means you are choosing life, dignity, and freedom. God does not want you to stay in a place of harm. *"The Lord is my helper; I will not be afraid. What can mere mortals do to me?"* (Hebrews 13:6)

Facing the Truth with Courage

Acknowledging that you are in an abusive relationship is one of the hardest steps, but it is also one of the most liberating.

The enemy uses fear and lies to keep you trapped, but God's truth will set you free.

- **Truth #1**: You are not to blame for the abuse. It is a choice made by the abuser, not a reflection of your worth.

- **Truth #2**: God sees your pain and is with you, even when you feel abandoned.

- **Truth #3**: There is a way out. It may take time and planning, but you are not powerless.

Prayer for Strength:
Lord, I feel so trapped and afraid, but I know You are with me. Give me the strength to see the truth about my situation and the courage to take steps toward freedom. Help me to trust that You have plans for my life—plans to prosper me and not harm me. Amen.

A Glimpse of Hope

This chapter is not just about recognizing the darkness; it's about seeing the light at the end of the tunnel. God has a plan for your escape and healing. As you move forward in this book, you will find practical guidance, spiritual encouragement, and hope to reclaim the life God intended for you—a life of peace, joy, and freedom.

"The Spirit of the Lord is on me, because he has anointed me to proclaim good news to the poor. He has sent me to proclaim freedom for the prisoners and recovery of sight for the blind, to set the oppressed free." (Luke 4:18)

Let this promise be your foundation as you prepare to break free from the chains of abuse. You are not alone, and you are stronger than you realize.

Chapter 2:

Building Your Confidence and Faith

Leaving an abusive relationship is not just a physical process—it's a spiritual and emotional one, too. Abuse erodes your sense of self and your confidence, making it harder to believe you can live a better life. In this chapter, we'll focus on rebuilding your self-esteem, grounding yourself in God's truth, and preparing emotionally and spiritually for the journey ahead. Faith is the cornerstone of this process, and as you strengthen your trust in God, you will find the courage to take the necessary steps toward freedom.

Reclaiming Your Identity in Christ

Abuse often attacks your identity, making you feel worthless or powerless. But your true worth is not defined by your abuser's words or actions—it is defined by God.

- **Who You Are in Christ**:

  - You are deeply loved (*"I have loved you with an everlasting love."* Jeremiah 31:3).

  - You are valuable (*"You are worth more than many sparrows."* Matthew 10:31).

  - You are chosen and set apart (*"You are a chosen people, a royal priesthood."* 1 Peter 2:9).

Take time to meditate on these truths. Speak them over yourself daily. Write them on sticky notes and place them where you can see them—on your mirror, refrigerator, or car dashboard.

Practical Exercise: Write a letter to yourself from God's perspective, focusing on how He sees you. Use scriptures to affirm His love for you.

Recognizing and Challenging Lies

Abusers often use lies to control and manipulate. Over time, these lies can become part of your inner dialogue. It's important to identify and replace them with God's truth.

- **Common Lies You May Believe**:

  - *Lie*: "This is my fault."

    - *Truth*: Abuse is never your fault. Your abuser chooses their actions.

    - *Scripture*: *"The Lord is close to the brokenhearted and saves those who are crushed in spirit."* (Psalm 34:18).

  - *Lie*: "I can't survive without them."

    - *Truth*: You are stronger than you realize, and God will provide for your needs.

    - *Scripture*: *"And my God will meet all your needs according to the riches of his glory in Christ Jesus."* (Philippians 4:19).

  - *Lie*: "No one will love me after this."

- *Truth*: God's love is unconditional, and He has plans to restore and bless you.

- *Scripture*: "The Lord your God is with you, the Mighty Warrior who saves. He will take great delight in you; in his love, he will no longer rebuke you, but will rejoice over you with singing."* (Zephaniah 3:17).

Practical Exercise: Make a list of lies you've believed and write a scripture-based truth to counter each one.

Daily Affirmations and Prayers for Strength

Affirmations grounded in scripture are powerful tools to rebuild your confidence and trust in God.

- **Affirmations to Declare Daily**:

  - "I am a child of God, and He loves me unconditionally."

  - "I am strong and courageous because God is with me."

  - "I have the power to make decisions that honor God and protect my peace."

  - "God is my refuge and strength; I am not alone."

- **Sample Prayer**:
Heavenly Father, I feel so small and unsure of myself, but I know that You are my strength. Help me to see myself through Your eyes—as someone precious, worthy, and loved. Remind me daily that I can do all things through Christ who strengthens me. Amen.

Seeking Wise Counsel

One of the most empowering steps you can take is reaching out for support. God often works through people, and wise counsel can provide clarity, encouragement, and resources to help you move forward.

- **Who to Reach Out To**:

  - Trusted friends or family members who support your safety and well-being.

  - Pastors or spiritual leaders who can provide biblical encouragement.

  - Professional counselors or therapists trained in trauma recovery.

  - Support groups for domestic violence survivors.

- **What to Say**:

  - Be honest about your situation. Share as much or as little as you're comfortable with.

  - Ask for specific help, whether it's prayer, a safe place to stay, or assistance finding resources.

Scripture Encouragement: *"Plans fail for lack of counsel, but with many advisers, they succeed."* (Proverbs 15:22)

Practical Steps to Rebuild Confidence

1. **Set Small, Achievable Goals**: Start with something manageable, like organizing important documents or calling

a support hotline. Each small success builds your confidence.

2. **Celebrate Your Strengths**: Reflect on moments when you showed courage or resilience, even if they seem small.

3. **Focus on Self-Care**: Prioritize activities that nurture your body, mind, and spirit, such as prayer, journaling, exercise, or spending time in nature.

Exercise: Create a "Confidence Journal." Each day, write down one thing you did well, one truth from scripture, and one thing you're grateful for.

Trusting God in the Process

It's natural to feel fear and uncertainty as you prepare to leave an abusive relationship. You may not see the full picture of what lies ahead, but trust that God is guiding you step by step.

*   **Biblical Example of Courage**:

    *   Consider the story of the Israelites fleeing Egypt. They didn't know how they would escape Pharaoh's army or cross the Red Sea, but God made a way. *"The Lord will fight for you; you need only to be still."* (Exodus 14:14)

    *   In the same way, God will make a way for you, even if it feels impossible.

Prayer for Courage:
Lord, I feel afraid of what lies ahead, but I know that You are my protector and provider. Help me to trust You even when I can't

see the full plan. Strengthen my faith and give me the courage to take the next step. Amen.

Facing the Future With Confidence

Rebuilding your confidence and faith is an ongoing journey. Each day that you choose to lean on God and take small steps forward is a victory. Remember that confidence doesn't mean never feeling fear—it means trusting God enough to act despite your fear.

As you strengthen your faith and rediscover your worth, you will find that you are not defined by your past or your pain. God has greater things in store for you—a life of freedom, peace, and purpose.

Scripture to Hold Onto: *"The Lord is my light and my salvation—whom shall I fear? The Lord is the stronghold of my life—of whom shall I be afraid?"* (Psalm 27:1)

Chapter 3:

Mapping Out a Safe Exit Plan

Leaving an abusive relationship is a process that requires careful planning and preparation, especially if you have children or limited resources. This chapter provides practical steps to create a comprehensive exit plan, ensuring your safety and setting the foundation for a secure future. It also includes spiritual encouragement and guidance to strengthen your resolve, reminding you that God is with you every step of the way.

The Importance of a Safe Exit

Deciding to leave an abusive relationship is one of the most courageous choices you can make, but it's also one of the most dangerous times. Statistics show that the risk of violence often escalates when a victim attempts to leave. This is why a well-thought-out exit plan is crucial.

Key Goals of an Exit Plan:

1. Protect yourself and your children from harm.

2. Secure essential documents and resources.

3. Establish a safe place to stay.

4. Build a network of support.

Step 1: Recognize Your Resources and Support System

Your first step is identifying the people and organizations that can help you. Remember, you don't have to do this alone.

- **Trusted People**:

  - Friends or family members who are supportive and discreet.

  - A pastor, counselor, or church leader who can provide spiritual and practical guidance.

  - Neighbors who can assist in emergencies.

- **Organizations and Hotlines**:

  - National Domestic Violence Hotline: 1-800-799-SAFE (7233)

  - Local shelters or domestic violence agencies.

  - Legal aid organizations for restraining orders or custody issues.

Scripture Encouragement: *"Two are better than one, because they have a good return for their labor: If either of them falls down, one can help the other up."* (Ecclesiastes 4:9-10)

Step 2: Gather Essential Documents and Items

Before leaving, collect important documents and items you'll need for your new life. Keep these in a safe place, such as with a trusted friend or in a storage locker.

- **Important Documents**:

  - Identification: IDs, birth certificates, Social Security cards.

  - Financial records: bank statements, pay stubs, credit cards.

  - Legal documents: marriage license, restraining orders, custody papers.

  - Medical records for you and your children.

- **Essential Items**:

  - Cash or prepaid debit cards (if possible, avoid using shared bank accounts).

  - Keys: house, car, storage unit.

  - Medications and health insurance cards.

  - A change of clothes for you and your children.

Practical Tip: Create a "go bag" with these items and keep it hidden or stored with someone you trust.

Step 3: Identify a Safe Destination

Having a secure place to go is critical. This could be a domestic violence shelter, the home of a trusted friend or family member, or even a hotel.

- **Choosing a Safe Place**:

  - Avoid places your abuser knows you frequent.

- If possible, stay in a location where your abuser cannot find you easily.

- Consider shelters that offer security and counseling services.

- **Plan Your Route**:

- Know how you will get to your destination.

- Keep a backup plan in case your initial route is blocked or unsafe.

Prayer for Guidance:
Lord, guide my steps as I prepare to leave. Show me the right place to go, and surround me with people who will protect and support me. Amen.

Step 4: Inform Authorities and Legal Professionals

If you fear for your safety, it's essential to involve law enforcement and seek legal protection.

- **Restraining Orders**: Obtain a protective order to keep your abuser away from you and your children.

- **Child Custody**: If you have children, consult a family lawyer to understand your rights and secure custody arrangements.

- **Police Assistance**: Inform local law enforcement about your situation. Many police departments have advocates trained to assist domestic violence victims.

Scripture Encouragement: *"The Lord is a refuge for the oppressed, a stronghold in times of trouble."* (Psalm 9:9)

Step 5: Secure Your Financial Independence

Abusers often use finances as a tool to control their victims. Gaining financial independence is a crucial step in your escape plan.

- **Open a Separate Bank Account**: If possible, open an account in your name at a bank your abuser doesn't use.

- **Build Emergency Savings**: Save small amounts of cash or gift cards over time.

- **Seek Employment or Education**: Look for job opportunities or training programs that can provide long-term stability.

- **Utilize Community Resources**: Many organizations offer financial assistance, job training, and housing support for domestic violence survivors.

Practical Tip: If you are unable to open a bank account or find work immediately, connect with local charities or churches that provide emergency aid.

Step 6: Prepare Your Children (If Applicable)

If you have children, their safety and well-being are paramount.

- **Age-Appropriate Conversations**:
  - Explain the situation in a way they can understand, emphasizing that you are keeping them safe.

- Avoid blaming or bad-mouthing the abuser in front of them.

- **Create a Safety Plan for Them**:

  - Teach them to call 911 in emergencies.

  - Have a code word that signals they need to leave with you immediately.

  - Pack their favorite toys or comfort items to ease the transition.

Prayer for Your Children:
Lord, protect my children as we prepare to leave. Surround them with Your peace and shield their hearts from fear. Help me to guide them with wisdom and love. Amen.

Step 7: Execute the Plan with Caution

When the time comes to leave, act swiftly and discreetly.

- **Choose the Right Time**: Leave when your abuser is away, asleep, or otherwise distracted.

- **Avoid Confrontation**: Do not inform your abuser of your plans directly. This could escalate the situation.

- **Have a Backup Plan**: If something goes wrong, know who to call or where to go for immediate help.

Scripture Encouragement: *"The name of the Lord is a fortified tower; the righteous run to it and are safe."* (Proverbs 18:10)

Step 8: Secure Your Safety After Leaving

After leaving, take steps to protect yourself and your children from further harm.

- **Change Contact Information**: Get a new phone number and email address. Block your abuser on social media.

- **Alert Key People**: Inform your workplace, children's school, and others in your life about the situation. Provide a copy of any restraining order.

- **Stay Vigilant**: Be cautious about sharing your location or returning to places your abuser may frequently visit.

Lean on God's Strength

The process of leaving may feel overwhelming, but God's strength is made perfect in your weakness. Trust Him to guide and protect you.

Prayer for Strength:
Father, as I take these steps to leave, I ask for Your protection and provision. Calm my fears, strengthen my resolve, and remind me that I am never alone. Thank You for being my refuge and deliverer. Amen.

Scripture to Hold Onto:

- *"Fear not, for I have redeemed you; I have summoned you by name; you are mine. When you pass through the waters, I will be with you."* (Isaiah 43:1-2)

- *"God is our refuge and strength, an ever-present help in trouble."* (Psalm 46:1)

This chapter equips you with the tools, steps, and faith you need to safely leave an abusive relationship. With God's guidance and the right resources, you can begin your journey toward freedom and healing.

Chapter 4:

Overcoming the Trauma

Leaving a domestic violence situation is a monumental step, but the journey to healing doesn't stop there. Trauma can linger long after the abuse has ended, affecting your mental, emotional, physical, and spiritual well-being. Overcoming the trauma requires intentional effort, patience, and faith as you rebuild your life. This chapter provides practical steps, spiritual guidance, and encouragement to help you move forward and find lasting healing.

Understanding Trauma

Trauma is the body and mind's response to overwhelming events, like abuse. It manifests in many ways, including:

- **Emotional Symptoms**: Anxiety, depression, guilt, shame, or emotional numbness.

- **Physical Symptoms**: Fatigue, headaches, muscle tension, or changes in sleep and appetite.

- **Mental Symptoms**: Flashbacks, difficulty concentrating, or intrusive thoughts.

- **Relational Symptoms**: Difficulty trusting others, fear of intimacy, or withdrawal from loved ones.

Understanding that these reactions are normal can be a powerful first step in overcoming trauma. Recognize that healing is not linear, and it's okay to have setbacks as you work through your pain.

Scripture Encouragement:
"He heals the brokenhearted and binds up their wounds." (Psalm 147:3)

Steps to Overcome Trauma

1. Seek Professional Help

Healing from trauma often requires professional support. Therapists, counselors, and support groups are invaluable resources.

- **Trauma-Focused Therapy**: Consider therapy methods like cognitive-behavioral therapy (CBT), eye movement desensitization and reprocessing (EMDR), or faith-based counseling.

- **Support Groups**: Connecting with others who have experienced similar struggles can help you feel less alone and provide mutual encouragement.

Practical Tip: Research local or online support resources, and don't hesitate to reach out for help.

2. Reclaim Your Emotional Health

Your emotions may feel overwhelming at times, but with time and effort, you can regain control.

- **Journaling**: Writing about your feelings can help you process them and release pent-up emotions.

- **Practice Self-Compassion**: Treat yourself with kindness and understanding, especially on hard days.

- **Learn Emotional Regulation**: Techniques like deep breathing, mindfulness, or prayer can help calm your mind and body during moments of distress.

Scripture Encouragement:
"Do not fear, for I am with you; do not be dismayed, for I am your God. I will strengthen you and help you; I will uphold you with my righteous right hand." (Isaiah 41:10)

3. Rebuild Your Identity

Trauma can strip away your sense of self-worth and identity. Reclaiming who you are is essential to healing.

- **Affirm Your Worth**: Replace negative self-talk with affirmations of God's truth about you.

  - *"I am loved." (Romans 8:38-39)*

  - *"I am fearfully and wonderfully made." (Psalm 139:14)*

  - *"I am a new creation in Christ." (2 Corinthians 5:17)*

- **Pursue New Interests**: Explore hobbies or activities that bring you joy and help you rediscover your passions.

- **Surround Yourself with Positive Influences**: Build relationships with people who encourage and uplift you.

Exercise: Write down three things you love about yourself or would like to rediscover about yourself.

4. Restore Your Spiritual Health

Faith is a powerful tool in overcoming trauma. Turning to God for healing can bring peace, comfort, and renewal.

- **Pray for Healing**: Talk to God openly about your pain and ask for His help in your healing journey.

- **Meditate on God's Word**: Focus on scriptures that remind you of His love, protection, and promises.

- **Participate in Worship and Community**: Being part of a church or spiritual group can strengthen your faith and provide valuable support.

Scripture Encouragement:
"Come to me, all you who are weary and burdened, and I will give you rest." (Matthew 11:28)

Prayer for Healing:
Lord, I bring my pain and brokenness to You. Heal my heart and mind, and give me the strength to move forward. Help me to trust in Your plan and rest in Your peace. Amen.

5. Take Care of Your Body

Trauma affects not only the mind but also the body. Prioritize physical self-care to aid in your recovery.

- **Exercise Regularly**: Physical activity can reduce stress and boost your mood.

- **Eat Nourishing Foods**: A balanced diet helps your body recover and supports overall health.

- **Rest and Relaxation**: Prioritize sleep and find time for activities that help you unwind.

Practical Tip: Develop a self-care routine that incorporates physical, emotional, and spiritual wellness.

Embracing Hope and the Future

Healing from trauma is a journey, not a destination. It's about progress, not perfection. As you take steps to overcome trauma, remember that God is with you every step of the way.

Key Truths to Hold Onto:

1. **Your Past Does Not Define You**: You are not your trauma or your abuse. You are a beloved child of God with a future filled with hope.

2. **Healing is Possible**: With time, effort, and faith, you can overcome even the deepest wounds.

3. **You Are Not Alone**: God walks with you, and there are people and resources ready to support you.

Scripture Encouragement:
"And the God of all grace, who called you to his eternal glory in Christ, after you have suffered a little while, will himself restore you and make you strong, firm, and steadfast." (1 Peter 5:10)

Final Prayer for Overcoming Trauma:
Heavenly Father, thank You for walking with me through the darkest moments of my life. Help me to release the pain of my past and embrace the healing You offer. Fill me with Your peace and remind me that I am never alone. Guide me as I continue to

grow, heal, and step into the future You have prepared for me. In Jesus' name, Amen.

Overcoming trauma is not easy, but it is possible. Each step you take is a testament to your strength and courage. Hold onto hope, trust in God's plan, and believe that a brighter, freer future is ahead.

Chapter 5:

Rebuilding a Life of Peace and Joy

Breaking free from domestic violence is a courageous and transformative step, but true freedom comes when you rebuild your life with peace and joy as its foundation. After surviving trauma, the challenge is to embrace a life of purpose and fulfillment. This chapter will guide you through practical and spiritual steps to create a stable, secure, and joyful future.

What Does a Life of Peace and Joy Look Like?

A life of peace and joy doesn't mean a life free of challenges, but it does mean:

- **Peace**: The absence of chaos and fear, replaced with a sense of security and calm.

- **Joy**: A deep, abiding sense of gratitude and contentment, even amid life's ups and downs.

Both peace and joy are gifts from God, but they require intentional effort to cultivate. It starts with renewing your mind, setting healthy boundaries, and building a future centered on faith and purpose.

Scripture Encouragement:
"The peace of God, which transcends all understanding, will guard your hearts and your minds in Christ Jesus." (Philippians 4:7)

Step 1: Creating a Safe and Stable Environment

Rebuilding begins with stability. A secure environment is essential for fostering peace and joy.

- **Establish a Safe Home**: Whether you're living on your own or with others, create a space that feels safe and nurturing. Decorate it with things that bring you comfort and joy, such as photos, art, or scripture.

- **Financial Independence**: Take steps to manage your finances. This may include creating a budget, seeking employment, or working with a financial advisor.

- **Routine and Structure**: Establish daily routines that give you a sense of control and purpose.

Practical Tip: Identify one area in your life where you can create more stability, such as organizing your home or planning your week.

Step 2: Building Healthy Relationships

A life of peace and joy is often rooted in healthy, supportive relationships.

- **Reconnect with Trusted People**: Rebuild relationships with friends and family who are uplifting and supportive.

- **Set Boundaries**: Learn to say no to relationships or situations that threaten your peace.

- **Seek Community**: Join groups or organizations, such as a church or hobby group, where you can connect with like-minded people.

Step 3: Cultivating Joy Through Gratitude

Gratitude is a powerful tool for restoring joy. It shifts your focus from what you've lost to what you have gained.

- **Practice Gratitude Daily**: Start a gratitude journal and write down three things you're thankful for each day.

- **Celebrate Small Wins**: Acknowledge and celebrate even the smallest achievements in your journey.

- **Find Joy in the Present**: Look for simple pleasures, like a beautiful sunset, a good meal, or a kind word from a friend.

Exercise: At the end of each day, reflect on one moment that brought you joy and thank God for it.

Step 4: Rediscovering Your Purpose

God has a unique purpose for your life, and discovering it can bring immense joy and fulfillment.

- **Seek God's Guidance**: Spend time in prayer and ask God to reveal His plan for your life.

- **Pursue Your Passions**: Reflect on what brings you joy and explore ways to incorporate those passions into your life.

- **Serve Others**: Helping others can bring a deep sense of purpose and connection.

Prayer for Purpose:
Lord, guide me as I rebuild my life. Show me the purpose You have for me and help me to live it out with courage and joy. Amen.

Step 5: Embracing Spiritual Growth

Your relationship with God is the foundation for lasting peace and joy.

- **Deepen Your Faith**: Spend time in prayer, study scripture, and worship regularly.

- **Forgive Yourself and Others**: Let go of bitterness and guilt, and allow God's grace to bring you peace.

- **Trust God's Plan**: Even when the future feels uncertain, trust that God is working all things for your good.

Scripture Encouragement:
"You make known to me the path of life; you will fill me with joy in your presence, with eternal pleasures at your right hand." (Psalm 16:11)

Living in Peace and Joy

Rebuilding a life of peace and joy is a journey, but with every step, you move closer to the life God intended for you.

- **Peace Comes From God**: Rest in the knowledge that God is your protector and provider.

- **Joy Comes From Within**: True joy is not dependent on circumstances but on your relationship with God and the gratitude in your heart.

- **You Are Worthy**: You deserve a life of peace, joy, and love.

Scripture Encouragement:
"The Lord gives strength to his people; the Lord blesses his people with peace." (Psalm 29:11)

Prayer for Peace and Joy:
Heavenly Father, thank You for bringing me through the storm and into a new season. Help me to rebuild my life on the foundation of Your love and promises. Fill my heart with peace and joy, and guide me as I walk forward in faith. In Jesus' name, Amen.

Rebuilding your life after domestic violence is not easy, but it is possible. With faith, determination, and support, you can create a future that reflects God's love and your incredible strength. Keep moving forward, one step at a time, and embrace the abundant life God has prepared for you.

Chapter 6:

Finding Fulfillment in Christ

After surviving the pain of domestic violence and beginning the journey to healing, it's natural to search for fulfillment—a sense of purpose and satisfaction that transcends your circumstances. True fulfillment can only be found in a relationship with Christ. In Him, you discover your identity, purpose, and the abundant life He promises.

This chapter will guide you in deepening your connection with Christ, understanding your God-given worth, and living a life of purpose, peace, and fulfillment.

Why Fulfillment Can Only Be Found in Christ

The world often defines fulfillment by external achievements—money, success, or relationships. However, these things are temporary and cannot heal the deep wounds left by trauma or provide lasting peace.

Fulfillment in Christ comes from knowing:

- **Who You Are**: You are a beloved child of God, created in His image.

- **Why You Are Here**: God has a purpose for your life, uniquely designed for you.

- **Where You Are Going**: Through Christ, you have the hope of eternal life.

Scripture Encouragement:
"I have come that they may have life, and have it to the full." (John 10:10)

Step 1: Deepening Your Relationship with Christ

The first step to finding fulfillment is cultivating a close, personal relationship with Jesus.

- **Spend Time in Prayer**: Prayer is your direct connection to God. Share your heart with Him—your fears, hopes, and gratitude.

- **Study God's Word**: The Bible is a guide for understanding who God is and how much He loves you.

- **Worship with Gratitude**: Praise God for His goodness, even in small moments. Worship aligns your heart with His.

Practical Tip: Start each morning with a quiet moment in prayer and scripture, asking God to guide your day.

Scripture Encouragement:
"Draw near to God, and He will draw near to you." (James 4:8)

Step 2: Embracing Your Identity in Christ

Abuse can strip away your sense of worth, leaving you feeling broken and unworthy. But in Christ, you are made whole and new.

- **You Are Loved**: God's love for you is unconditional and eternal.

- **You Are Forgiven**: No matter your past, Christ's sacrifice covers all sins.

- **You Are Redeemed**: Your pain does not define you; God can use it to shape a beautiful future.

Exercise: Write down three scriptures that remind you of your worth in Christ. Reflect on them daily.

Scripture Encouragement:
"Therefore, if anyone is in Christ, the new creation has come: The old has gone, the new is here!" (2 Corinthians 5:17)

Step 3: Living Out Your Purpose

God created you with a unique purpose that only you can fulfill. Finding and pursuing that purpose brings deep fulfillment.

- **Ask God for Guidance**: Pray for clarity about the gifts and passions He has placed in your heart.

- **Serve Others**: Fulfillment often comes from helping others. Look for opportunities to serve in your community or church.

- **Trust God's Timing**: God's purpose unfolds step by step. Be patient and trust His plan.

Scripture Encouragement:
"For we are God's handiwork, created in Christ Jesus to do good works, which God prepared in advance for us to do." (Ephesians 2:10)

Step 4: Resting in God's Peace

Fulfillment in Christ also means finding peace in Him, regardless of life's circumstances.

- **Let Go of Control**: Surrender your worries and plans to God, trusting that He knows what is best.

- **Forgive and Release**: Forgiveness is not for your abuser—it's for you. Letting go of anger and bitterness frees your heart.

- **Anchor Yourself in God's Promises**: When fear or doubt arises, remind yourself of God's faithfulness.

Prayer for Peace:
Lord, I surrender my fears and burdens to You. Fill my heart with Your peace that surpasses understanding and help me to trust Your plan for my life. Amen.

Scripture Encouragement:
"You will keep in perfect peace those whose minds are steadfast, because they trust in You." (Isaiah 26:3)

Step 5: Experiencing True Joy in Christ

Joy is not the absence of hardship but the presence of Christ in your life. When you walk with Him, joy becomes your strength.

- **Celebrate the Little Things**: Gratitude turns ordinary moments into blessings.

- **Choose Joy Daily**: Joy is a choice. Focus on God's goodness instead of your circumstances.

- **Share Your Testimony**: Telling others how God has transformed your life can deepen your own sense of joy.

Scripture Encouragement:
"The joy of the Lord is your strength." (Nehemiah 8:10)

Living a Fulfilled Life in Christ

Fulfillment in Christ is an ongoing journey. It's about trusting Him daily, leaning on His strength, and finding joy in His presence.

Key Truths to Remember:

1. **You Are Not Alone**: Christ walks with you every step of the way.

2. **You Have a Purpose**: Your life has meaning and value in God's plan.

3. **You Are Free**: In Christ, you are no longer bound by your past.

Scripture Encouragement:
"Now to Him who is able to do immeasurably more than all we ask or imagine, according to His power that is at work within us, to Him be glory in the church and in Christ Jesus throughout all generations, for ever and ever! Amen." (Ephesians 3:20-21)

Prayer for Fulfillment in Christ:
Heavenly Father, thank You for Your unfailing love and for the hope I have in You. Help me to walk daily in Your purpose for my life, filled with Your peace and joy. Teach me to trust You fully and to find my ultimate fulfillment in Your presence. Amen.

Through Christ, you can find the peace, joy, and fulfillment that surpass all understanding. You were created for more—more love, more purpose, more life. Step into the fullness of what God has for you and live the abundant life He promises.

Conclusion

A New Beginning in Freedom and Faith

As you reach the final pages of this book, remember that your journey does not end here. In fact, it is just the beginning. You've taken brave and powerful steps to break free from the chains of abuse, heal from trauma, and embrace a life filled with peace, joy, and purpose. This journey is not just about surviving; it's about thriving in every area of your life—mentally, emotionally, spiritually, physically, and financially.

The path you have walked has been difficult, but it has also been transformative. Every tear, every prayer, and every small victory has brought you closer to the person God created you to be. As you move forward, hold tightly to the truths you've learned: you are deeply loved by God, you are worthy of respect and safety, and you have the strength to create a beautiful, fulfilling life.

Reflecting on the Journey

Take a moment to reflect on how far you've come:

1. **You've Found Your Voice**: You refused to let fear silence you. You spoke up, sought help, and took action to protect yourself and, if applicable, your children.

2. **You've Rediscovered Your Worth**: You now understand that your value comes from God, not from anyone's opinion or treatment of you.

3. **You've Built a Foundation for Healing**: You've committed to doing the hard work of healing, growing, and trusting God with your pain.

4. **You've Stepped Into Freedom**: You've left behind the darkness of abuse and stepped into a life of hope, love, and possibility.

Scripture Encouragement:
"Forget the former things; do not dwell on the past. See, I am doing a new thing! Now it springs up; do you not perceive it? I am making a way in the wilderness and streams in the wasteland." (Isaiah 43:18-19)

The Power of Faith and Action

Faith has been the cornerstone of your journey, and it will continue to sustain you in the days to come. It was your faith that gave you the courage to leave, the strength to heal, and the vision to dream of a better life.

But faith alone is not enough; it must be paired with action. You have demonstrated this by taking practical steps to protect yourself, create a plan, and rebuild your life. Keep this partnership between faith and action at the forefront of everything you do.

Practical Encouragement: As you continue your journey, make a habit of praying about your decisions and taking steps, no matter how small, to move forward in God's purpose for your life.

Living in Freedom

Freedom is not just a destination; it is a way of life. It means choosing daily to walk in peace, joy, and security, regardless of life's challenges. It means rejecting fear, guilt, and shame and embracing your identity as a child of God.

- **Celebrate Your Strength**: You are stronger than you ever imagined. Take pride in the fact that you have overcome tremendous adversity and emerged as a victor.

- **Be Gracious With Yourself**: Healing is not linear, and there may still be difficult days ahead. Allow yourself grace and time to grow.

- **Trust God's Plan**: Even when the future seems uncertain, rest in the assurance that God is guiding your steps.

Scripture Encouragement:
"The Lord makes firm the steps of the one who delights in him; though he may stumble, he will not fall, for the Lord upholds him with his hand." (Psalm 37:23-24)

Encouragement for the Future

Your journey is a testimony to others who are still trapped in darkness. By living your life with courage, faith, and purpose, you can be a light to those who need hope. Whether through your words, actions, or simple presence, you have the power to inspire and uplift others.

Prayer for the Journey Ahead:

Heavenly Father, thank You for walking with me every step of the way. Help me to continue to grow, heal, and live in Your purpose. Use my life as a testimony of Your love and faithfulness. Strengthen me for the journey ahead and fill me with Your peace, joy, and security. Amen.

The road you have traveled was never meant to break you but to shape you into the resilient, courageous, and beautiful person you are today. God has taken your pain and is turning it into purpose. He has taken the ashes of your past and is creating something new and beautiful.

As you close this book, hold onto these truths:

- You are loved.

- You are worthy.

- You are strong.

- You are free.

Scripture to Carry Forward:

"For I know the plans I have for you," declares the Lord, "plans to prosper you and not to harm you, plans to give you hope and a future." (Jeremiah 29:11)

Go forward with confidence, knowing that God is with you, guiding you into a future filled with peace, joy, and security. Your best days are ahead. Walk boldly into the life God has prepared for you, and never forget you are more than a survivor—you are victorious.

Renewing

YOUR MIND FOR SUCCESS

30 DAY DEVOTIONAL JOURNAL

Welcome to Renewing Your Mind for Success, a 30-day devotional journal designed to help you align your thoughts, actions, and goals with God's Word.

Success is often defined by the world in terms of wealth, status, or achievements. However, as followers of Christ, true success begins within— a transformation of the mind that allows us to see and pursue God's purpose for our lives.

The Bible calls us to be "transformed by the renewing of your mind" (Romans 12:2). This means shifting our focus away from worldly pressures and distractions, and instead, filling our minds with God's truth. By doing so, we allow His wisdom, peace, and guidance to lead us in every area of life, including our personal, spiritual, and professional pursuits.

Each day of this journal will guide you through scripture-based insights and reflection, challenging you to let go of limiting beliefs, replace negative thoughts with God's promises, and step into the success He has already planned for you. These devotions are not just about achieving success as the world defines it, but about discovering the fullness of God's plan for your life and using your gifts for His glory.

As you walk through these 30 days, I encourage you to take time to reflect deeply, pray earnestly, and invite God to transform your mind. You may experience challenges or setbacks, but remember that God is working in and through you, even in the waiting. Let each day's scripture and reflection renew your faith, build your confidence, and draw you closer to the Lord, knowing that He has great things in store for you.

Are you ready to step into the renewed mind God desires for you? Let's begin this journey of transformation and success—together with Him.

Dr. Latina C. Campbell

Romans 12:2 – "Do not conform to the pattern of this world, but be transformed by the renewing of your mind. Then you will be able to test and approve what God's will is—his good, pleasing and perfect will."

True success begins in the mind. Renewing your thoughts transforms how you perceive challenges, opportunities, and God's will for your life. Reflection: What thoughts are holding you back from God's best?

DAY 2: ALIGNING YOUR THOUGHTS WITH GOD'S WORD

Philippians 4:8 – "Finally, brothers and sisters, whatever is true, whatever is noble, whatever is right... think about such things."

What we dwell on shapes our actions. Align your thoughts with what is true, noble, and right for success that honors God.
Reflection: Are my thoughts aligned with God's truth? What do I think about?

DAY 3: CASTING DOWN NEGATIVE THOUGHTS

Corinthians 10:5 – "We demolish arguments and every pretension that sets itself up against the knowledge of God..."

Negative thoughts hinder your progress. Cast them down and replace them with God's promises.
Reflection: What negative thoughts are limiting my potential?

DAY 4: GOD'S VISION FOR SUCCESS

Jeremiah 29:11 – "For I know the plans I have for you..."

God's vision for success involves peace and prosperity for His children.
Trust His plans for you.
Reflection: Do I believe God has good plans for my success?

DAY 5: OVERCOMING FEAR

2 Timothy 1:7 – "For God has not given us a spirit of fear, but of power..."

Fear can cripple progress. Overcome fear by leaning into the power and love God gives.
Reflection: What fear is stopping me from moving forward?

DAY 6: THE IMPORTANCE OF FAITH

Hebrews 11:1 – "Now faith is confidence in what we hope for..."

Success in God's Kingdom requires faith—believing in what
you cannot yet see.
Reflection: Where do I need to exercise more faith?

DAY 7: SPEAKING LIFE AND BLESSINGS

Proverbs 18:21 – "The tongue has the power of life and death..."

Your words carry power. Speak life over your goals, dreams, and plans.

Reflection: Am I speaking words of life or death over my situation?

DAY 8: SEEKING GOD'S WISDOM

James 1:5 – "If any of you lacks wisdom, you should ask God..."

True success comes from seeking and applying God's wisdom.

Reflection: Have I been seeking God's wisdom in my decisions?

James 1:2-3 – "Consider it pure joy... when you face trials... because you know that the testing of your faith produces perseverance."

Success often involves challenges. Embrace trials as opportunities to grow.

Reflection: How can I view current trials as preparation for success?

Matthew 6:33 – "But seek first his kingdom and his righteousness…"

When you focus on God and His righteousness, He will align everything else for your good.
Reflection: Where am I prioritizing other things over God?

Luke 16:10 – "Whoever can be trusted with very little can also be trusted with much..."

God rewards faithfulness in the small tasks. When you show diligence and responsibility in the little things, He opens doors for greater opportunities.

Reflection: How can I demonstrate more faithfulness in the small things?

DAY 12: ABIDING IN CHRIST FOR SUCCESS

John 15:4-5 – "Remain in me, as I also remain in you... apart from me
you can do nothing."

Lasting success comes from abiding in Christ. Without Him, we labor in
vain. Stay connected to the source of true strength and wisdom.
Reflection: Am I trying to achieve success in my own strength, or am I
abiding in Christ?

DAY 13: RELEASING CONTROL TO GOD

Proverbs 3:5-6 – "Trust in the Lord with all your heart and lean not on your own understanding..."

Success comes from trusting God's plans and surrendering control.
Release your need to figure everything out, and trust that God is directing your steps.
Reflection: Where do I need to release control and trust God more fully?

DAY 14: GOD'S TIMING IS PERFECT

Ecclesiastes 3:11 – "He has made everything beautiful in its time..."

While we often want immediate results, God's timing is perfect. Trust Him to bring success in the right season.
Reflection: Have I been impatient in waiting for God's timing?

_____

_____

_____

_____

_____

_____

_____

_____

_____

_____

DAY 15: WALKING IN OBEDIENCE

Deuteronomy 28:1 – "If you fully obey the Lord your God and carefully follow all his commands... the Lord your God will set you high above all the nations on earth."

Obedience to God's Word is key to unlocking His blessings and success in our lives.
Reflection: Is there any area of disobedience hindering my success?

DAY 16: LETTING GO OF PAST FAILURES

Isaiah 43:18-19 – "Forget the former things; do not dwell on the past
See, I am doing a new thing!"

Dwelling on past failures can hold you back. God is always doing something
new. Let go of past mistakes and embrace the new opportunities He is
preparing for you.

Reflection: Am I holding on to past failures that are keeping me from moving
forward?

DAY 17: THE ROLE OF PRAYER IN SUCCESS

1 Thessalonians 5:17 – "Pray continually."

Prayer is essential in seeking God's guidance and blessings. Regular communication with God strengthens your faith and aligns your desires with His will.
Reflection: How can I make prayer a more consistent part of my pursuit of success?

DAY 18: DILIGENCE AND HARD WORK

Proverbs 10:4 – "Lazy hands make for poverty, but diligent hands brir wealth."

Success requires diligence and hard work. God blesses those who work diligently and put their hands to the task.
Reflection: In what areas do I need to be more diligent?

DAY 19: SOWING AND REAPING

Galatians 6:9 – "Let us not become weary in doing good, for at the proper time we will reap a harvest if we do not give up."

Success doesn't come overnight. It's a process of sowing good seeds consistently and waiting patiently for the harvest.
Reflection: What seeds am I sowing today that will lead to success in the future?

Revelation 3:8 – "See, I have placed before you an open door that no o[n]e can shut..."

When God opens a door, no one can shut it. Trust that He is the one who creates opportunities for your success.
Reflection: Am I recognizing the doors God is opening for me, or am I focuse[d] on closed ones?

DAY 21: HUMILITY LEADS TO HONOR

Proverbs 22:4 – "Humility is the fear of the Lord; its wages are riches and honor and life."

Humility is a key ingredient in Godly success. The more we humble ourselves, the more God lifts us up in honor and success.
Reflection: In what areas of my life do I need to practice more humility?

DAY 22: WALKING IN PEACE

Philippians 4:7 – "And the peace of God, which transcends all understanding, will guard your hearts and your minds in Christ Jesus.

Success without peace is incomplete. Seek the peace of God that goes beyond understanding, even in the midst of busy or challenging seasons.
Reflection: Am I pursuing peace in my journey toward success?

DAY 23: THE POWER OF VISION

Proverbs 29:18 – "Where there is no vision, the people perish..."

A clear vision provides purpose and direction. Pray for God's vision for your life and success, and follow it faithfully.
Reflection: Have I sought God's vision for my life and success?

DAY 24: RESTING IN GOD'S PROMISES

Matthew 11:28-30 — "Come to me, all you who are weary... and I will gi
you rest."

Success requires periods of rest. Rest in God's promises, knowing that He is
working even when you are still.'
Reflection: Have I been striving without taking time to rest in God?

DAY 25: SURROUNDING YOURSELF WITH WISE COUNSEL

Proverbs 15:22 – "Plans fail for lack of counsel, but with many advisers they succeed."

Surround yourself with wise, Godly counsel to ensure success in your plans and decisions.

Reflection: Do I seek wise counsel for my decisions, or am I trying to do it all alone?

Proverbs 11:25 – "A generous person will prosper; whoever refreshes others will be refreshed."

Success in God's Kingdom involves being a blessing to others. When you refresh others, you too will be refreshed.
Reflection: How can I be a blessing to those around me today?

DAY 27: GRATITUDE AND CONTENTMENT

Philippians 4:11-13 – "I have learned to be content whatever the circumstances…"

True success is not measured by material wealth but by a heart of gratitude and contentment in every situation.
Reflection: Am I living with gratitude and contentment, or am I chasing things that don't satisfy?

DAY 28: STANDING FIRM IN YOUR IDENTITY

Ephesians 2:10 – "For we are God's handiwork, created in Christ Jesus do good works, which God prepared in advance for us to do."

Your identity in Christ is foundational to your success. Knowing who you are in Him gives you the confidence to step boldly into your calling.
Reflection: Am I standing firm in my identity as a child of God, or am I seeking validation from the world?

DAY 29: PERSEVERING TOWARD THE GOAL

Philippians 3:14 – "I press on toward the goal to win the prize for which God has called me heavenward in Christ Jesus."

Success in God's Kingdom is not a destination, but a journey of continual perseverance. We are called to press on, regardless of the challenges we face, knowing that the ultimate prize is not earthly success, but fulfilling God's purpose for our lives. Keep your eyes fixed on the eternal goal, trusting that every step, every challenge, and every victory is leading you closer to the ultimate reward in Christ.

Reflection: What goals do I need to keep pressing toward, trusting God to help me persevere?

DAY 30: LIVING FOR GOD'S GLORY

1 Corinthians 10:31 – "So whether you eat or drink or whatever you do,
it all for the glory of God.

At the end of the day, true success is about living for God's glory. Every action
every achievement, and every step forward should point back to Him.
Reflection: Am I pursuing success for my glory or for God's glory?